My English Book 3

and Me!

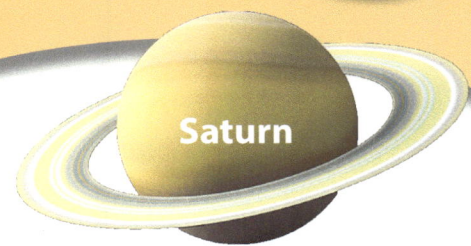

Saturn

I'm

_____.
name

I'm

_____.
years old

My
birthday is

_____
month

_____.
day

I go to

_____.
school

I'm in grade

_____

Today is

_____
month _____
day _____.
year

ISBN 9781-939729-02-6

Printed in Japan

Table of Contents

e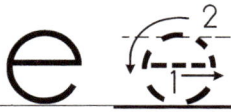

         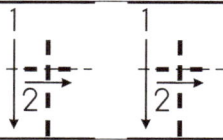

___ gg   ___ lephant   ___ leven   ___ ggplant

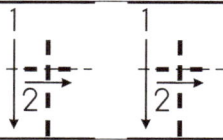   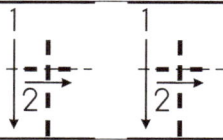

___ able   ___ omato   ___ en   ___ ea

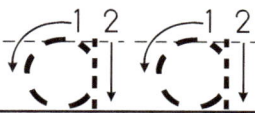   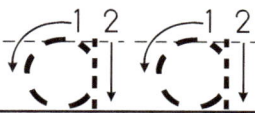

___ nt   ___ pple   ___ lligator   ___ x

4

Name: _____ **Date:** _____

_____ gg   _____ nt   _____ able   _____ leven

_____ ea   _____ lligator   _____ pple   _____ x

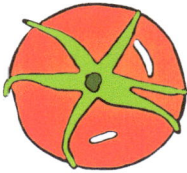  

_____ omato   _____ en   _____ ggplant   _____ lephant

_____ elevision   _____ npanman   _____ levator   _____ elephone

Score:	Date:	Comment:
_____ / 16		
_____ / 16		
_____ / 16		

Name: _____ **Date:** _____

_____ pple   _____ en   _____ ent   _____ gg

_____ rain   _____ nt   _____ omato   _____ iger

_____ leven   _____ lligator   _____ able   _____ urtle

_____ ggplant   _____ merica   _____ lephant   _____ oothbrush

Score:	Date:	Comment:
_____ / 16		
_____ / 16		
_____ / 16		

What's your name?

I'm _____.

How old are you?

I'm _____.

Name: _____ **Date:** _____

_____ x

_____ scalator

_____ npanman

_____ elephone

_____ ree

_____ ea

_____ gg

_____ leven

_____ urtle

_____ eddy bear

_____ lephant

_____ merica

_____ nt

_____ oothbrush

_____ ggplant

_____ iger

Score:	Date:	Comment:
_____ / 16		
_____ / 16		
_____ / 16		

Name: _____   **Date:** _____

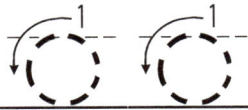

_____ n   _____ ff   _____ range   _____ ctopus

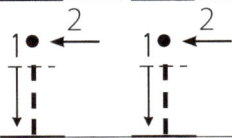

_____ nsects   _____ gloo   _____ n   _____ nk

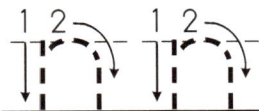

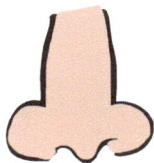   

_____ ose   _____ uts   _____ inja   _____ ine

Name: _____ **Date:** _____

_____ ine

_____ nk

_____ n

_____ range

_____ n

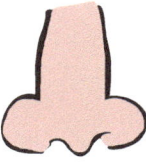

_____ ose

_____ uts

_____ gloo

_____ ff

_____ ctopus

_____ nsects

_____ inja

_____ guana

_____ est

_____oodles

p_____ t

Score:	Date:	Comment:
_____ / 16		
_____ / 16		
_____ / 16		

Name: _____   **Date:** _____

n   t   a   e   i   o   u

_____ ose   _____ omato   _____ nt   _____ scalator

_____ uts   _____ range   _____ ctopus   _____ nsects

_____ ea   _____ gloo   _____ pple   _____ gg

_____ _____ st   _____ n   _____ eddy bear   _____ _____ t

Score:	Date:	Comment:
_____ / 18		
_____ / 18		
_____ / 18		

What's your name?

I'm _____.

How old are you?

I'm _____.

When's your birthday?

It's _____.

n   t   a   e   i   o   u

11

_____ leven _____ merica _____ npanman _____ nsect

   **9**

_____ n _____ _____ nt _____ ea _____ ine

_____ nja _____ ff _____ gloo _____ ctopus

  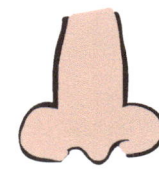

_____ nk _____ ggplant _____ x _____ ose

Score:	Date:	Comment:
_____ / 18		
_____ / 18		
_____ / 18		

Name: _____ **Date:** _____

a   e   i   o

c____t   p____n   f____x   b____g

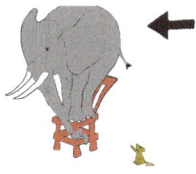   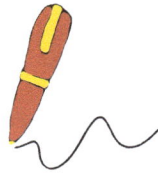      

b____g   p____n   d____g   s____ck

n____st   p____t   p____n   b____x

t____nt   t____n   n____t   s____x

Score:	Date:	Comment:
____ / 16		
____ / 16		
____ / 16		

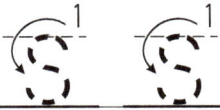

_____ ock   _____ ix   _____ even   _____ un

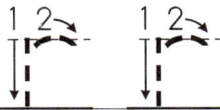

  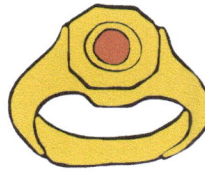 

_____ ed   _____ abbit   _____ ing   _____ ain

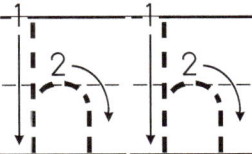 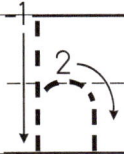

_____ orse   _____ ouse   _____ at   _____ and

Name: _____ **Date:** _____

_____

_____ ed

_____

_____ ix

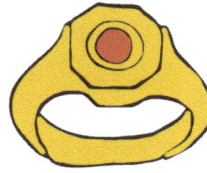

_____

_____ ing

_____

_____ and

_____

_____ even

_____

_____ ouse

_____

_____ ock

_____

_____ orse

_____

_____ ain

_____

_____ abbit

_____

_____ at

_____

_____ un

_____

_____ nake

_____

_____ elicopter

_____

_____ ippo

_____

_____ ocket

Score:	Date:	Comment:
_____ / 16		
_____ / 16		
_____ / 16		

16

Name: _____ **Date:** _____

h   n   r   s   t   a   e   i   o

_____

_____ ouse

_____

_____ ain

_____

_____ ainbow

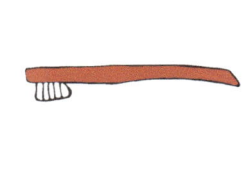
_____

_____ oothbrush

_____

_____ lligator

_____

_____ ven

_____

_____ lephant

_____

_____ range

_____

_____ orse

_____

_____ _____ x

_____

_____ un

_____

_____ nsects

_____

_____ ine

_____

_____ d

_____

_____ _____ t

_____

_____ eart

Score:	Date:	Comment:
_____ / 20		
_____ / 20		
_____ / 20		

What's your name?

I'm _____.

When's your birthday?

It's _____.

How old are you?

I'm _____.

What's your favorite color?

I like _____.

18

Name: _____ **Date:** _____

h   n   r   s   t   a   e   i   o

____ ____ bbit

____ ____ ck

____ x

____ ggplant

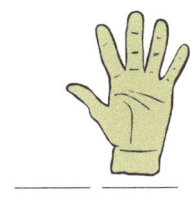

____ ____ nd

____ ____ ndwich

____ un

____ n

____ ouse

____ guana

____ able

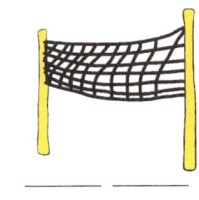

____ ____ t

____ elephone

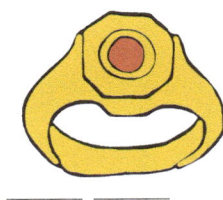

____ ____ ng

____ elicopter

____ bot

Score:	Date:	Comment:
____ / 23		
____ / 23		
____ / 23		

_____

____ nk   _____ t   ____ ctopus   ____ ain

_____

_____ x   ____ uts   ____ gloo   ____ urtle

_____

____ mbulance   ____ strich   ____ ven   ____ eart

 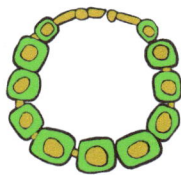  

_____

____ ainbow   ____ ecklace   ____ ain   ____ scalator

Score:	Date:	Comment:
_____ / 20		
_____ / 20		
_____ / 20		

Name: _____ **Date:** _____

a	e	i	o

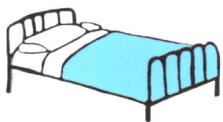
b____d

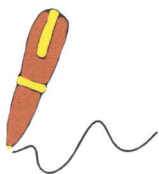
p____n

b____x

n____t

p____t

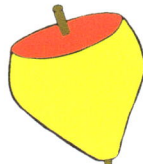
t____p

s____x

m____p

b____t

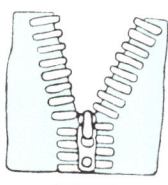
p____n

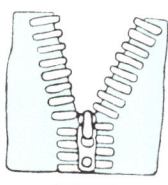
z____p

t____n

m____t

h____t

r____d

y____n

Score:	Date:	Comment:
____ / 16		
____ / 16		
____ / 16		

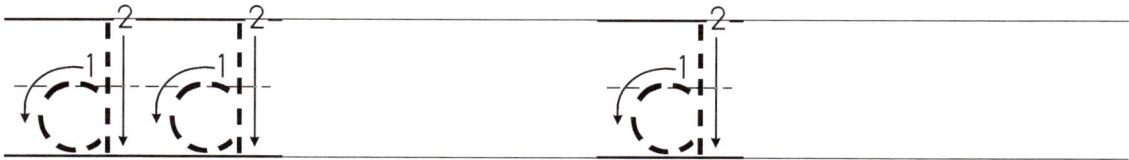

_____ uck   _____ oor   _____ esk   _____ og

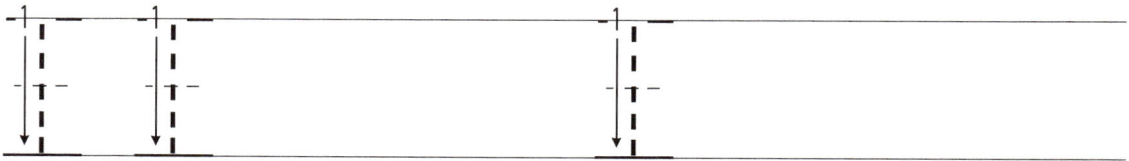

_____ amp   _____ eg   _____ ion   _____ emon

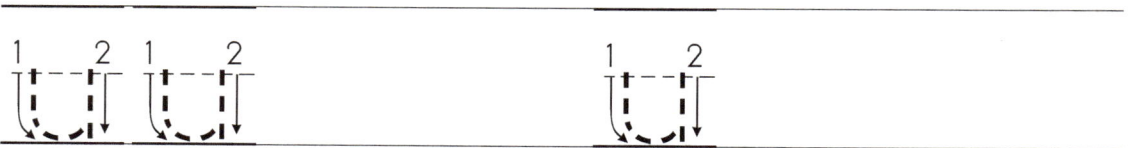

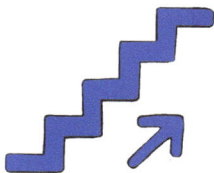   

_____ p   _____ nder   _____ gly   _____ mbrella

_____ og

_____ emon

_____ ion

_____ p

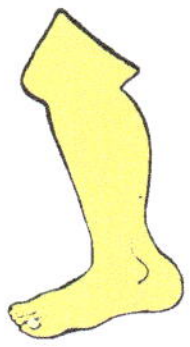

_____ eg

_____ esk

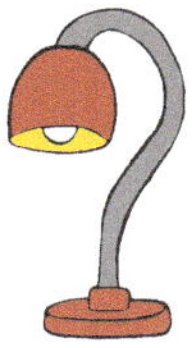

_____ amp

_____ mbrella

_____ nder

_____ uck

_____ gly

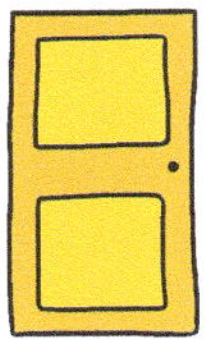

_____ oor

_____ olphin

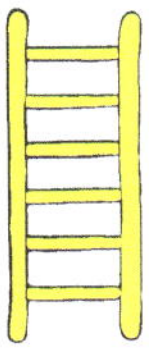

_____ adder

_____ inosaur

c____ p

Score:	Date:	Comment:
_____ / 16		
_____ / 16		
_____ / 16		

Name: _____ **Date:** _____

d   h   l   n   r   s   t   a   e   i   o   u

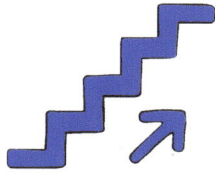

____ p

____ eaf

____ olphin

____ adybug

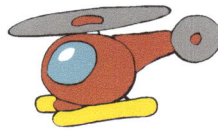

____ iamond

____ elicopter

6

____ x

____ amburger

____ ____ cket

____ bot

____ oodles

____ nsects

____ strich

____ mbulance

____ ree

____ levator

Score:	Date:	Comment:
____ / 19		
____ /19		
____ / 19		

24

What's your name?

I'm _____.

How old are you?

I'm _____.

When's your birthday?

It's _____.

What's your favorite color?

I like _____.

What's your favorite fruit?

I like _____.

Name: _____ **Date:** _____

d   h   l   s   a   e   i   o   u

___ mbrella   ___ ion   ___ inosaur   ___ ___ mburger

___ npanman   ___ gg   ___ ___ g   ___ mon

h___ t d___ g   ___ ___ ven   ___ nake   ___ nk

___ ___ ndwich   ___ guana   ___ merica   ___ lephant

Score:	Date:	Comment:
___ / 22		
___ / 22		
___ / 22		

Name: _____ **Date:** _____

d l n r t a e i o u

_____

_____ nder

_____

_____ mp

_____

_____ ainbow

_____

_____ ddy bear

_____

_____ t

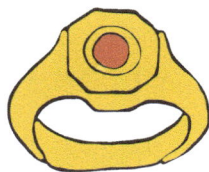
_____

_____ ng

_____

_____ omato

_____

_____ adybug

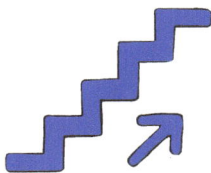
_____

_____ p

_____

_____ oor

_____

_____ _____ st

_____

_____ ff

_____

_____ n

_____

_____ onut

_____

_____ _____ d

_____

_____ urtle

Score:	Date:	Comment:
_____ / 22		
_____ / 22		
_____ / 22		

Name: _____   **Date:** _____

d h l n r s t a e i o u

____ mbrella

____ ____ g

____ sk

____ ____ n

____ range

____ iger

____ ggplant

____ ck

____ gly

____ ppo

____ mon

____ bbit

____ eart

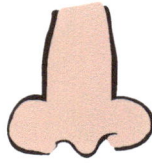

____ ose

____ gloo

____ lligator

Name: _____ **Date:** _____

a   e   i   o   u

   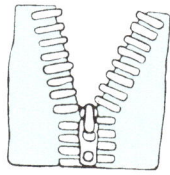      

b____ x   z____ p   s____ ck   b____ s

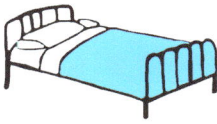         

b____ d   m____ p   r____ d   p____ nk

b____ t   h____ t d____ g   s____ n   t____ b

m____ p   y____ n   d____ g   c____ t

Score:	Date:	Comment:
____ / 17		
____ / 17		
____ / 17		

Name: _____ **Date:** _____

____ arrot   ____ ake   ____ at   ____ ar

   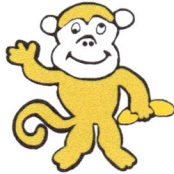      

____ oon   ____ onkey   ____ ouse   ____ elon

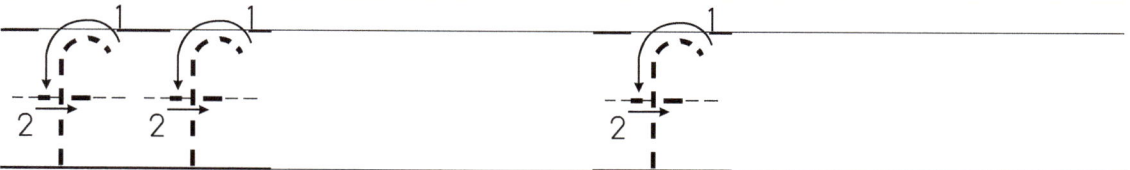

____ ish   ____ ork   ____ our   ____ ive

_____

_____ our

_____

_____ ar

_____

_____ ouse

_____

_____ ake

_____

_____ oon

_____

_____ ive

_____

_____ onkey

_____

_____ ish

_____

_____ at

_____

_____ arrot

_____

_____ elon

_____

_____ ork

_____

_____ up

_____

_____ ow

_____

_____ ilk

_____

_____ ox

Score:	Date:	Comment:
_____ / 16		
_____ / 16		
_____ / 16		

Name: _____ **Date:** _____

c d f h l m r a e i o u

   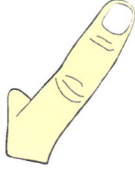   

_____ _____   _____ _____   _____ _____   _____ _____

_____ shroom   _____ _____ nger   _____ g   _____ _____ g

_____ _____   _____ _____   _____ _____   _____ _____

_____ nster   _____ og   _____ ow   _____ ain

   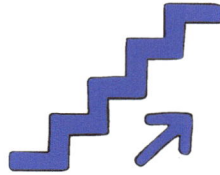      

_____   _____   _____   _____

_____ ookie   _____ p   _____ ion   _____ ck

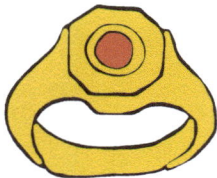         

_____ _____   _____   _____   _____

_____ _____ ng   _____ nd   _____ ouse   _____ _____ cket

Score:	Date:	Comment:
_____ / 26		
_____ / 26		
_____ / 26		

What's your name?

I'm _____.

How old are you?

I'm _____.

When's your birthday?

It's _____.

What's your favorite color?

I like _____.

What's your favorite vegetable?

I like _____.

What's your favorite fruit?

I like _____.

Name: _____ **Date:** _____

b c d f m n r t a e i o u

____ on____ t   ____ oon   ____ ____ sk   ____ ____ ng

____ ____ t   ____ onkey   ____ ____ sh   ____ ake

____ cklace   ____ ctopus   ____ ea   ____ ork

c____ p   b____ s   ____ ____ st   ____ bbit

Score:	Date:	Comment:
____ / 24		
____ / 24		
____ / 24		

34

Name: _____ **Date:** _____

c f h l m s a e i o u

_____ ar

_____ ouse

_____ our

_____ ppo

_____ mp

_____ leven

_____ mbulance

_____ guana

_____ arrot

_____ _____ lon

_____ ive

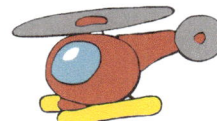
_____ _____ licopter

_____ eaf

_____ nake

_____ pider

_____ nt

Score:	Date:	Comment:
_____ / 20		
_____ / 20		
_____ / 20		

Name: _____ **Date:** _____

c d f h l m r a e i o u

_____ _____ nster

_____ ork

_____ orse

_____ emon

_____ ow

_____ oon

_____ r _____ g

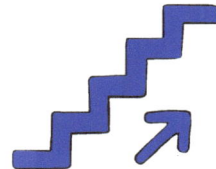

_____ p

_____ inosaur

_____ _____ t

_____ ainbow

_____ ion

_____ ake

_____ mbrella

_____ oor

_____ bot

Score:	Date:	Comment:
_____ / 20		
_____ / 20		
_____ / 20		

Name: _____ **Date:** _____

c　　f　　m　　n　　s　　t　　a　　e　　i　　o　　u

_____

_____ _____ t

_____

_____ _____ sh

_____

_____ _____ ts

_____

_____ ck

_____

_____ ookie

_____

_____ nsects

_____

_____ amurai

_____

_____ elevision

_____

_____ onkey

_____

_____ nger

_____ _____ nja

_____

_____ n

_____

_____ ushroom

_____

_____ range

_____

_____ iger

_____

_____ pple

Score:	Date:	Comment:
_____ / 22		
_____ / 22		
_____ / 22		

a   e   i   o   u

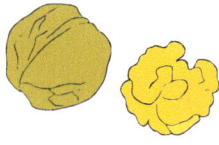   

n____ ts   m____ g   c___ t   c____ p

c____ p   d___ g   d____ ck   t____ nt

 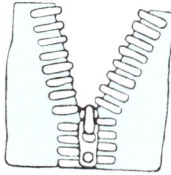  

v____ n   z___ p   y___ n   b____ x

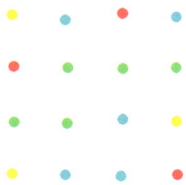  

d____ ts   b___ ll   h___ t d___ g   p___ n

Score:	Date:	Comment:
____ / 17		
____ / 17		
____ / 17		

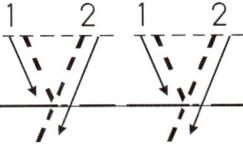

  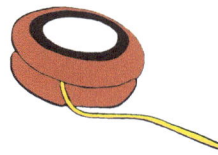 

_____ ellow   _____ ogurt   _____ o-yo   _____ acht

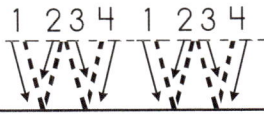   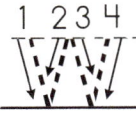

   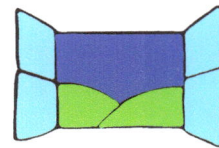

_____ hite   _____ hale   _____ atch   _____ indow

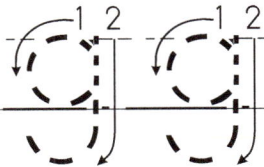   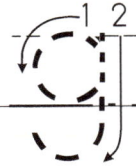

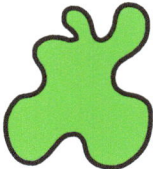 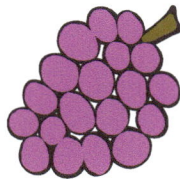  

_____ reen   _____ rapes   _____ orilla   _____ irl

Name: _____ **Date:** _____

_____ acht

_____ hite

_____ hale

_____ orilla

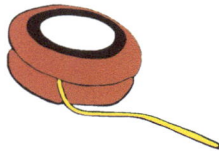

_____ o-yo

_____ atch

_____ irl

_____ ogurt

_____ ellow

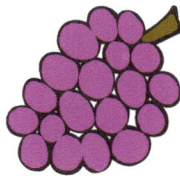

_____ rapes

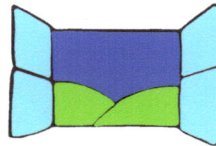

_____ indow

_____ reen

_____ en

_____ ater

_____ uitar

_____ randma

Score:	Date:	Comment:
_____ / 16		
_____ / 16		
_____ / 16		

Name: _____ **Date:** _____

b c f g l m w y a e i o u

_____ _____ n

_____ tch

_____ acht

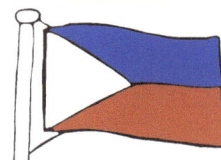
_____ l _____ g

_____ r _____ g

_____ ndy

_____ g

_____ dder

_____ oat

_____ aterm _____ lon

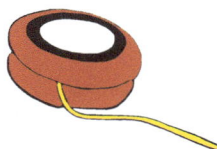
_____ o-yo

_____ _____ lon

_____ outh

_____ arrot

_____ _____ s

_____ adyb _____ g

Score:	Date:	Comment:
_____ / 27		
_____ / 27		
_____ / 27		

What's your name?

I'm _____.

How old are you?

I'm _____.

When's your birthday?

It's _____.

What's your favorite vegetable?

I like _____.

What's your favorite color?

I like _____.

What's your favorite fruit?

I like _____.

What's your favorite day?

I like _____.

Name: _____ **Date:** _____

d h n p r s t a e i o u

____ ____ ll

h____t d____g

____ ____ d

____ ainy

____ mbulance

____ oothbrush

____ oodles

____ n

____ g

____ ice

____ c____ssors

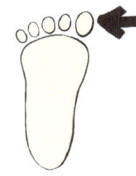

____ oe

____ oad

____ murai

____ ewspaper

____ merica

Score:	Date:	Comment:
_____ / 23		
_____ / 23		
_____ / 23		

Name: _____ **Date:** _____

c f g h l s w a e i o u

____ atch   ____ ____ x   ____ ____ t   ____ g

____ aterm ____ lon   ____ adyb ____ g   ____ air   ____ andwich

____ ____ n   ____ ____ t   ____ orse   ____ nake

____ n   ____ npanman   ____ ____ ligator ____ ____ gplant

Score:	Date:	Comment:
____ / 25		
____ / 25		
____ / 25		

Name: _____ **Date:** _____

d g m n r s t y a e i o u

_____

_____ _____ n

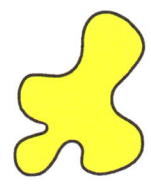

_____

_____ _____ llow

_____

_____ ck

_____

_____ ck

_____

_____ orilla

_____

_____ ogurt

_____

_____ ly

_____

_____ ice

_____

_____ rapes

_____

_____ ilk

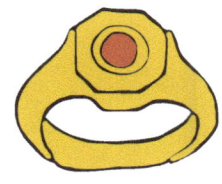

_____

_____ ng

_____

_____ cklace

_____

_____ ango

_____

_____ ug

_____

_____ oor

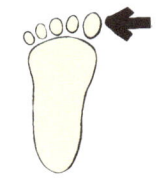

_____

_____ oe

Score:	Date:	Comment:
_____ / 23		
_____ / 23		
_____ / 23		

Name: _____ **Date:** _____

c d f g h l m n r s w y a e i o u

_____ _____ llow

_____ ive

_____ irl

_____ tch

_____ onkey

_____ p

_____ mbrella

_____ ion

_____ iamond

_____ mburger

_____ d

_____ x

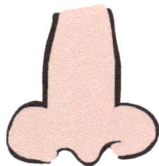

_____ ose

_____ gloo

_____ ctopus

_____ pple

Score:	Date:	Comment:
_____ / 22		
_____ / 22		
_____ / 22		

46

Name: _____ **Date:** _____

c d f g h l m p r t w y a e i o u

_____   _____   _____   _____

_____ ctopus   _____ ligator   _____ ddybear   _____ ephant

_____   _____   _____   _____

_____ rapes   _____ hite   yo-_____ o   _____ our

_____   _____   _____   _____

_____ oon   _____ ar   _____   _____ adyb_____ g

_____   _____   _____   _____

_____ sk   _____ licopter   _____ oad   _____ eaf

Score:	Date:	Comment:
_____ / 23		
_____ / 23		
_____ / 23		

Name: _____ **Date:** _____

a	e	i	o	u

  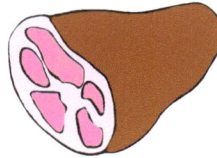 

h____t d____g　　h____n　　　　h____m　　　　j____g

j ____ g　　　　j ____ t　　　　m ____ p　　　　m ____ p

 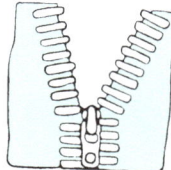  

y____n　　　　z____p　　　　r____ck　　　　r____d

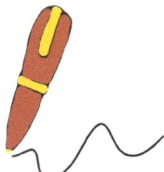  

p____n　　　　p____n　　　　p____n　　　　p____nk

Score:	Date:	Comment:
_____ / 17		
_____ / 17		
_____ / 17		

Name: _____ **Date:** _____

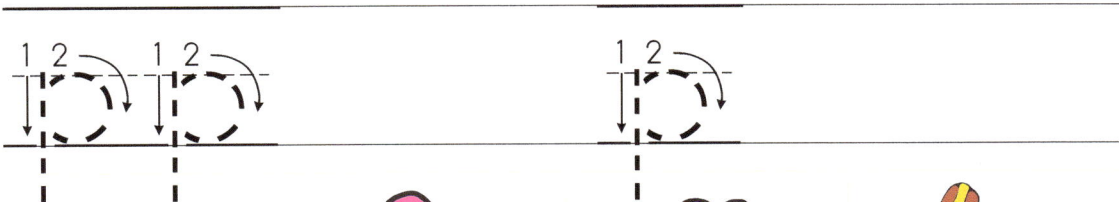

 _____ anda

 _____ ink

 _____ urple

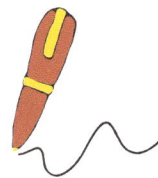 _____ en

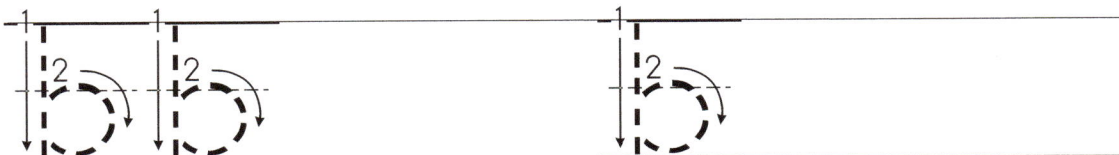

 _____ all

 _____ ag

 _____ ook

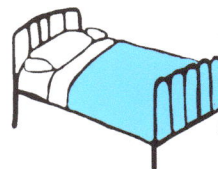 _____ ed

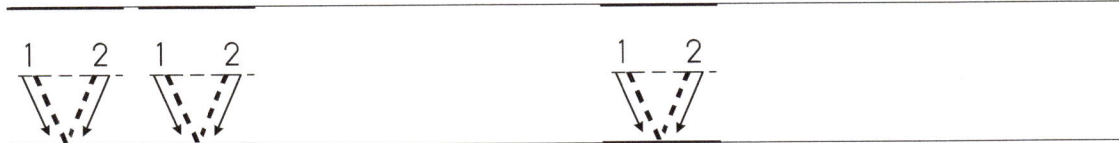

 _____ egetables

 _____ an

 _____ iolin

 _____ acuum

_____ iolin   _____ ook   _____ an   _____ urple

_____ egetables   _____ all   _____ ed   _____ anda

_____ en   _____ acuum   _____ ag   _____ ink

_____ ineapple   _____ at   _____ ig   _____ utterfly

Score:	Date:	Comment:
_____ / 16		
_____ / 16		
_____ / 16		

Name: _____   **Date:** _____

_____ _____ zza   _____ aby   _____ olcano   _____ r_____ndma

 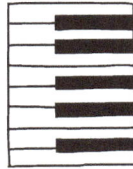  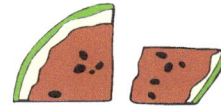

_____ r_____ndpa   _____ iano   _____ _____ s   _____ aterm_____ lon

_____ nguin   _____ nana   _____ ase   _____ acht

 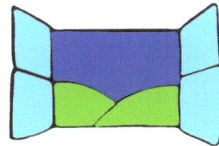  

_____ n   _____ ndow   _____ hale   _____ oat

Score:	Date:	Comment:
_____ / 25		
_____ / 25		
_____ / 25		

What's your name?

I'm _____.

How old are you?

I'm _____.

When's your birthday?

It's _____.

What's your favorite vegetable?

I like _____.

What's your favorite color?

I like _____.

What's your favorite fruit?

I like _____.

What's your favorite sport?

I like _____.

What's your favorite day?

I like _____.

Name: _____ **Date:** _____

d   h   l   n   r   s   t   a   e   i   o   u

_____ _____ dder   _____ _____ cket   _____ _____ t   _____ ree

_____ air   _____ nake   _____ ewspaper   _____ _____ bot

_____ _____ mp   _____ olphin   _____ inosaur   _____ _____ t

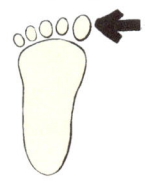
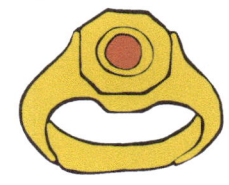

_____ pider   _____ ecklace   _____ oe   _____ _____ ng

Score:	Date:	Comment:
_____ / 23		
_____ / 23		
_____ / 23		

Name: _____ **Date:** _____

b c f g m p v w y a e i o u

_____ aby

_____ n

_____ ogurt

_____ _____ t

_____ _____ d

_____ reen

_____ getables

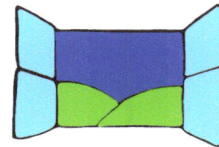

_____ ndow

_____ acuum

_____ _____ t

_____ r _____ ndma

_____ n

_____ ater

_____ n

_____ _____ x

_____ _____ lk

Score:	Date:	Comment:
_____ / 27		
_____ / 27		
_____ / 27		

b c g h n p s v y a e i o u

_____ _____ ase   _____ uitar   _____ urple   _____ _____ llow

_____ ewspaper   _____ _____licopter   _____ _____mburger   _____ olcano

_____ _____ t   _____ ee   _____ uzzle   _____ r_____ ndpa

_____ o-yo   _____ omputer   _____ orn   _____ ee-saw

Score:	Date:	Comment:
_____ / 21		
_____ / 21		
_____ / 21		

Name: _____ **Date:** _____

b c d f g h l m p v w y a e i o u

_____ _____getables   _____ izza   _____ ork   _____ sk

_____ acuum   _____ ook   _____ enguin   _____ acht

_____ ear   _____ orilla   _____ atermelon   _____ ouse

_____ ake   _____ mbrella   _____ adyb_____ g   _____ orse

Score:	Date:	Comment:
_____ / 19		
_____ / 19		
_____ / 19		

56

Name: _____ **Date:** _____

b c d f h l m n p r s t v a e i o u

_____ alloon

_____ nk

_____ eesaw

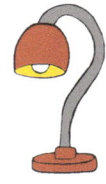

_____ mp

_____ ase

_____ g

_____ oad

_____ ow

_____ olcano

_____ nda

_____ ree

_____ ine

_____ ppo

_____ olphin

_____ onkey

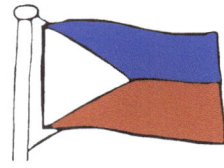

_____ l ___ g

Score:	Date:	Comment:
_____ / 22		
_____ / 22		
_____ / 22		

Name: _____ **Date:** _____

a   e   i   o   u

      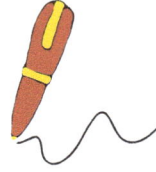   

h___ppo   h___t d___g   p___n   p___n

p___n   r___g   r___d   l___g

l___p   fl___g   fr___g   c___p

c___p   t___nt   ___x   s___d

Score:	Date:	Comment:
____ / 17		
____ / 17		
____ / 17		

58

Name: _____ **Date:** _____

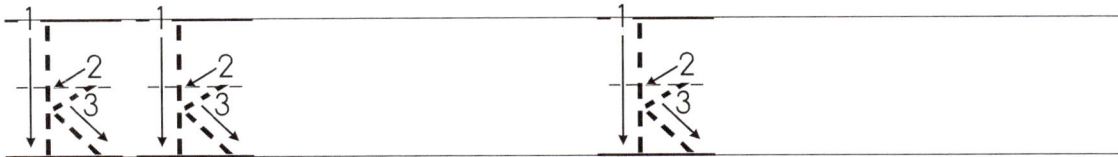

_____ oala

_____ angaroo

_____ ey

_____ ite

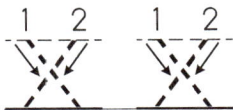

bo _____

fo _____

_____ -ray

_____ ylophone

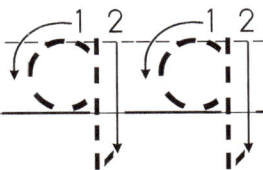

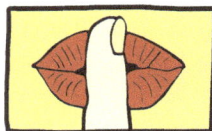

_____ uiet

_____ ueen

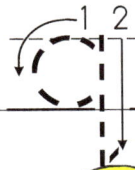

_____ uestion

earth _____ uake

_____

_____ ite

_____

bo _____

_____

_____ oala

_____

earth _____ uake

_____

_____ ueen

_____

_____ -ray

_____

_____ angaroo

_____

s _____ uare

_____

_____ ylophone

_____

_____ uestion

_____

_____ ey

_____

soc _____

_____

_____ uiet

_____

fo _____

_____

duc _____

_____

_____ etchup

Score:	Date:	Comment:
_____ / 16		
_____ / 16		
_____ / 16		

Name: _____ **Date:** _____

b g k p q v w x a e i o u

___iwi

s___ ___

___ueen

___ roccoli

___ ater

___ r___ndpa

m___

___ hale

___ ck

___ ineapple

___ ird

___ ase

___ ___ ss

___ u___ stion

___ irate

___ acuum

Score:	Date:	Comment:
___ /22		
___ / 22		
___ / 22		

What's your name?

I'm _____.

How old are you?

I'm _____.

When's your birthday?

It's _____.

What's your favorite vegetable?

I like _____.

What's your favorite color?

I like _____.

What's your favorite fruit?

I like _____.

What's your favorite sport?

I like _____.

What's your favorite day?

I like _____.

Can you swim?

Yes, I can./ No, I can't.

Name: _____ **Date:** _____

b f g k p q s v w x a e i o u

____ueen

____-ray

____o____

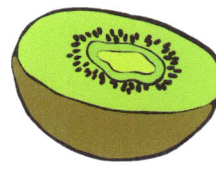
____iwi

____utterfly

____opcorn

____tch

____r____ndpa

____u____stion

____i____

____ey

____olcano

____iolin

____icycle

____otato

____r____ndma

Score:	Date:	Comment:
____ / 22		
____ / 22		
____ / 22		

Name: _____ **Date:** _____

c d f h l m n r s a e i o u

_____ _____ _____ _____

____ cklace   ____ murai   ____ ice   ____ t

_____ _____ _____ _____

____ now   ____ ck   ____ ppy   ____ ll

_____ _____ _____ _____

____ eaf   ____ p   ____ ainy   ____ onster

  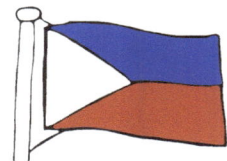

_____ _____ _____

____ dder   ____ elon   ____ r ____ g   ____ l ____ g

Score:	Date:	Comment:
____ / 26		
____ / 26		
____ / 26		

64

Name: _____ **Date:** _____

b g l m r s v x y a e i o u

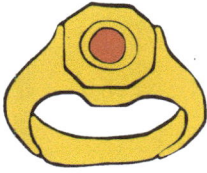
___ ___

___ ___

___ ___

___ ___

___ ___ ng

m ___ ___ ___

___ icycle

___ ___ ___ n

___ ___

___ ___

___ ___

___ ___

___ c ___ ssors

___ ___ ___ mon

___ irl

___ olcano

___ ___

___ ___

___ ___

___ ___

___ ___ ___ d

___ ion

___ ushroom

___ oat

___ ___

___ vase ___ ___
ase

___ ___

___ -ray

___ ___

___ ee

___ ase

___ -ray

___ ___ llow

Name: _____ **Date:** _____

c d f k n r p q w a e i o u

____ ____ ts

____ ____ ss

____ ookie

____ n

____ ____ ck

____ ____ t

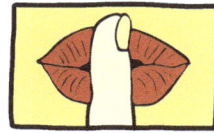
____ uiet

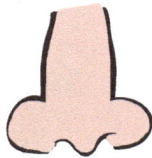
____ ork

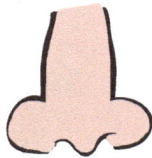
____ ose

____ ck

____ oor

____ ____ p

____ ____ x

____ hale

____ oala

____ pcorn

Score:	Date:	Comment:
____ / 25		
____ / 25		
____ / 25		

Name: _____   **Date:** _____

b g k m p v w x y a e i o u

____ ogurt   ____ otato   ____ getables   ____ i ____

____ ndy   ____ u ____ tar   ____ zza   ____ all

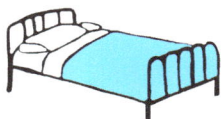

____ d   ____ olcano   ____ ____ ss   ____ randma

6   ¥

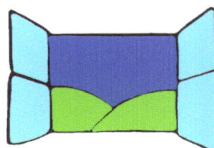

s ____ ____   ____ n   ____ ndow   ____ ____ ck

Score:	Date:	Comment:
____ / 27		
____ / 27		
____ / 27		

Name: _____ **Date:** _____

a	e	i	o	u

_____ _____ _____ _____

___ mbrella   ___ ff   ___ strich   ___ n

_____ _____ _____ _____

_____ nk   _____ gg   _____ nt   p _____ nda

_____ _____ _____ _____

_____ n   b ___ s   b _____ ll   b_____ g

 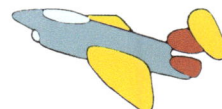

_____ _____ _____ _____

h____t d____g   w ___ g   s____ ck   j ____ t

Score:	Date:	Comment:
_____ / 17		
_____ / 17		
_____ / 17		

68

Name: _____ **Date:** _____

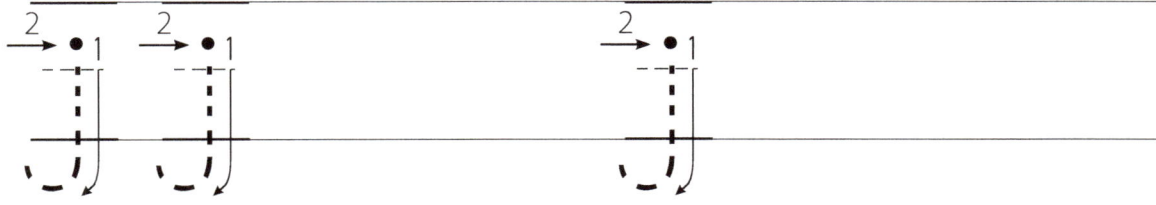

____ uice   ____ acket   ____ am   ____ ump rope

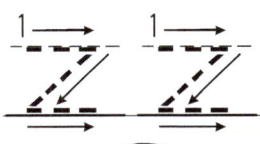 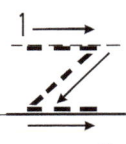

 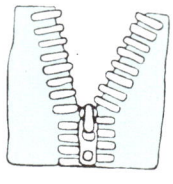  

____ ero   ____ ip   ____ ebra   ____ oo

Name: _____ **Date:** _____

_____ uice   _____ am   _____ ero   _____ et

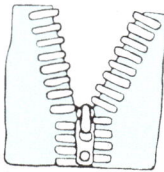  

_____ ip   _____ oo   _____ igzag   _____ udo

_____ ump rope   _____ ebra   _____ acket   _____ apan

_____ ar   _____ ump   _____ uggle   _____ aguar

Score:	Date:	Comment:
_____ / 16		
_____ / 16		
_____ / 16		

What's your name?

I'm _____.

How old are you?

I'm _____.

When's your birthday?

It's _____.

What's your favorite vegetable?

I like _____.

What's your favorite color?

I like _____.

What's your favorite fruit?

I like _____.

What's your favorite sport?

I like _____.

What's your favorite day?

I like _____.

Can you ski?

Yes, I can./ No, I can't.

Can you swim?

Yes, I can./ No, I can't.

Name: _____ **Date:** _____

b j k l q r v x z a e i o u

  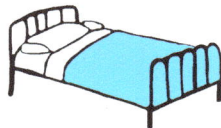 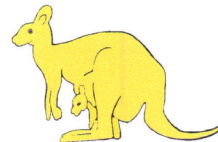

____ ____ m   ____ adybug   ____ ____ d   ____ angaroo

____ ebra   ____ ueen   ____ o ____   ____ ____ n

____ ____ t   ____ ero   ____ u ____ stion   ____ ____ tchup

  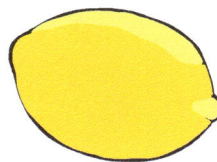 

____ ____ getables   ____ ____ g   ____ ____ mon   ____ ____ bbit

Score:	Date:	Comment:
____ / 27		
____ / 27		
____ / 27		

Name: _____ **Date:** _____

f g j m p w y z a e i o u

_____ pcorn

_____ udo

_____ ig_____ ag

_____ _____ ndy

_____ ushroom

_____ oo

_____ urple

_____ n

_____ _____ mp rope

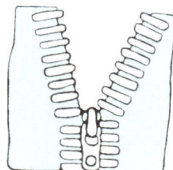

_____ _____ p

_____ _____ nk

_____ reen

_____ atermelon

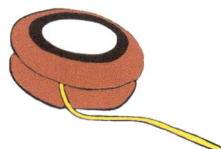

_____ o-yo

_____ _____ sh

_____ m

Score:	Date:	Comment:
_____ / 25		
_____ / 25		
_____ / 25		

Name: _____ **Date:** _____

c   d   h   j   n   r   s   t   a   e   i   o   u

      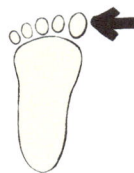   

_____   _____   _____   _____

____ ppy   ____ nake   ___ oe   ____ cket

_____   _____   _____   _____

____ nja   ____ ain   ____ ndle   ____ inosaur

_____   _____   _____   _____

____ pan   ____ omputer   ____ oor   ____ t

_____   _____   _____   _____

____ ine   ____ ice   ___ t ___ p   ____ elevision

Score:	Date:	Comment:
_____ / 23		
_____ / 23		
_____ / 23		

74

_____ gg   _____ utterfly   _____ n   _____ otato

_____ _____ ndow   _____ izza   _____ ushroom   _____ mp rope

_____ ase   _____ guar   _____ lligator   _____ range

_____ _____ mp   _____ gly   _____ ilk   _____ roccoli

Score:	Date:	Comment:
_____ / 20		
_____ / 20		
_____ / 20		

Name: _____ **Date:** _____

___ ebra   ___ o ___   _____ nk   ___ ppo

___ alloon   ___ oala   ___ ___mp rope   ___ ake

___ ey   ___ pan   ___ urtle   ___ ainbow

___ ion   ___ inosaur   ___utterfly   ___ hale

Score:	Date:	Comment:
___ / 21		
___ / 21		
___ / 21		

____atch

____iolin

____oodles

____ lon

____ ____d

____ ____nk

____ ____llow

____ hite

____ ____tter

____range

____ion

____o ____

____reen

____scalator

____ ____ven

____oon

Score:	Date:	Comment:
____ / 23		
____ / 23		
____ / 23		

___ iolin	___ bbit	___ ike	___ t___ p
_____ ___ mp	___ urple	___ i ___	___ ___ nja
___ mbrella	___ randma	___ mel	___ p
___ ctopus	___ now	___ gloo	___ otato

Score:	Date:	Comment:
_____ / 23		
_____ / 23		
_____ / 23		

_____ _____ rain

_____ aby

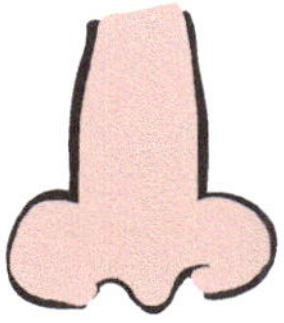

_____ ose

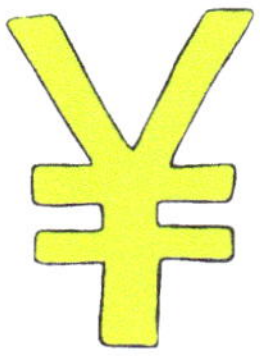

_____ n

_____ rapes

_____ arrot

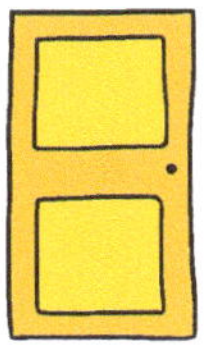

_____ oor

_____ uice

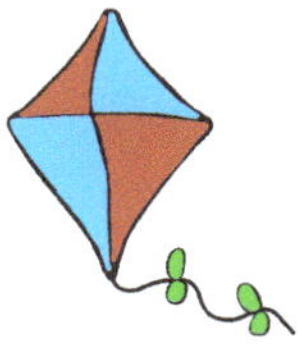

_____ ite

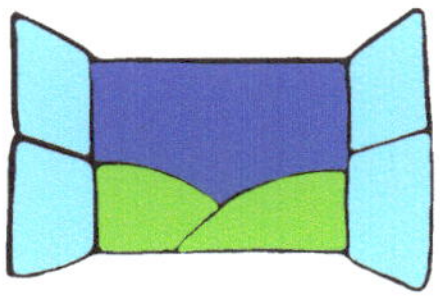

_____ ndow

_____ ebra

_____ ggplant

_____ _____ n

_____ amburger

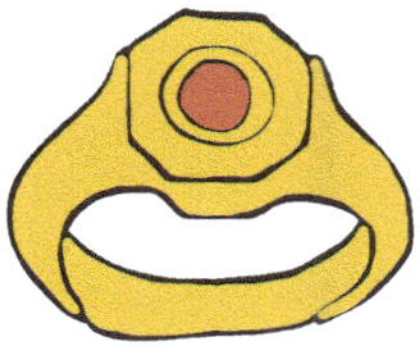

_____ _____ ng

_____ eaf

Score:	Date:	Comment:
_____ / 20		
_____ / 20		
_____ / 20		

Today is

month

day

year .

I'm _____ years old.

I'm in grade_____.

80